Catholic AND Cornered

Answers to Common Questions **About Your Faith**

Kenneth L. Parker

Foreword by Francis J. Beckwith

Liguori
ONE LIGUORI DRIVE
LIGUORI MO 63057-9999

Imprimi Potest:
Harry Grile, CSsR, Provincial
Denver Province, The Redemptorists

Published by Liguori Publications
Liguori, Missouri 63057

To order, call 800-325-9521
www.liguori.org

Library of Congress Cataloging-in-Publication Data
Parker, Kenneth L.
  Catholic and cornered : answers to common questions about your faith /
Kenneth L. Parker. -- 1st ed.
    p. cm.
  ISBN 978-0-7648-2025-0
  1. Catholic Church--Apologetic works--Miscellanea. I. Title.
  BX1752.P27 2011
  230'.2--dc22
                        2011012286

Scripture texts in this work are taken from the *New American Bible, revised edition*
© 2010, 1991, 1986, 1970 Confraternity of Christian Doctrine, Inc., Washington,
DC. All Rights Reserved.

Liguori Publications, a nonprofit corporation, is an apostolate of the
Redemptorists. To learn more about the Redemptorists, visit Redemptorists.com.

Printed in the United States of America
15 14 13 12 11   5 4 3 2 1

First Edition

Contents

Questions About the Priesthood

Questions About Monasticism and Vocational Life

Questions About the Sacraments

Questions About Worship

Questions About Catholic Devotions

Questions About Mary

Questions About Morality

Questions About Catholic Teaching

Conclusion ... 93

Where do I go from here? ... 95

Foreword

Wen I left the Catholic Church in my early teens, Evangelical Protestantism had all the answers to questions about the authority of Scripture, the nature of the Church, and what was necessary for salvation. Evangelicalism offered a coherent and attractive alternative to what I had been taught as a Catholic. So when I drifted away from the Church, I didn't see myself as leaving Christianity so much as moving to a tradition that seemed far more theologically serious than what I had encountered as a young, 1970s, post–Vatican II, American Catholic.

I later discovered that so much of what drew me to evangelicalism was Catholic—it was just in forms and practices seemingly foreign to me. My knowledge of Catholic thought, theology, and history was grossly superficial, and I had in effect not been properly catechized in my twelve years of parochial school. Thus, when I first encountered Evangelicals, their churches, their literature, and their theology, I wasn't properly prepared to critically assess them from a Catholic perspective. And given what I had learned as a Catholic about Christ, Scripture, and the triune Godhead, Evangelicalism didn't seem all that strange because it holds views consistent with Nicene Christianity.

Everything I came to substantively believe about Catholicism during my years of intellectual and spiritual formation as an Evangelical came from Protestant authors. Some were deeply hostile toward Catholicism, while others were critical but appreciative. In that sense, I was the typical Evangelical Protestant ex-Catholic who could play the personal-authority card when confronted by Catholic friends confused by my pilgrimage: "As a former Catholic...." I had uncritically accepted a Protestant account of Catholicism and uncritically believed it. Given my catechesis, I had no reason to think otherwise.

For instance, in my early twenties I led a group Bible study. Each week I taught and led discussion on an issue, Scripture passage, or theological question. I recently took a look at the notes I used for a session on Catholicism and realized what an embarrassment those notes are. My Catholic elementary and secondary education gave me a veneer of intellectual authority to spout inanities about Catholicism that, in reality, I had gleaned from well-meaning Protestant writers. I was convinced they were giving me real insight, and while I thought I had a competent grasp of Catholic thought and theology, I did not.

So when I first began seriously reading Catholic thought in my mid thirties and reconsidered Catholicism in my mid forties, I was surprised to learn how much I didn't know. I finally began to appreciate the depth and sophistication of the case for Catholicism, and this helped lead me back to the Church of my baptism in 2007.

For this reason, I am delighted about the publication of this book. Professor Kenneth Parker, an accomplished scholar of historical theology, has composed just the sort of learned and readable guide that explains the Catholic faith that I wish I had encountered in my youth. Like me, Professor Parker is a former Protestant who sees his conversion to Catholicism as a fulfillment—not repudiation—of the Evangelical chapter of his Christian journey. He writes as someone who has struggled with these questions not only as a scholar, but as a believer seeking to follow Christ as authentically as possible.

If you are a non-Catholic Christian—especially if, like me, you were baptized Catholic as an infant, I invite you to seriously consider the case Professor Parker makes in this book. So much of what you already believe and practice as a follower of Christ, whether you realize it or not, is deeply rooted in the historic Catholic Church—from the doctrine of the Trinity to salvation by grace to the deity of Christ and even the inspiration and authority of Scripture.

These and many other beliefs and practices were the result of the Holy Spirit moving in the Church to establish them as centerpieces of Christian orthodoxy. And, as I came to learn, that very Church also embraced and engaged in Catholic beliefs and practices I had thought, and you may currently think, are "unbiblical": the sacrament of confession, the real presence of Christ in the Eucharist, apostolic succession, purgatory, and the communion of saints.

Don't shy away from thinking carefully about issues that both unite and divide Catholics and Protestants. But do so with an open mind and a teachable spirit. After all, we are instructed by no less an authority than Jesus of Nazareth:

> *You shall love the Lord, your God,*
> *with all your heart, with all your soul,*
> *and with all your mind.*
> MATTHEW 22:37

FRANCIS J. BECKWITH
PROFESSOR OF PHILOSOPHY & CHURCH-STATE STUDIES
BAYLOR UNIVERSITY
58TH PRESIDENT OF THE EVANGELICAL THEOLOGICAL SOCIETY

Introduction

Most Catholics have been cornered by non-Catholics asking questions about the Church and the Catholic faith. To them, you are the spokesperson for the Catholic Church and are expected to have the answers to a wide range of complicated and difficult matters. Many of these queries would baffle everyday Catholics, an experienced catechist, or even your pastor.

I've been on both sides of these conversations. As one who was raised Protestant and became Catholic after years of theological studies, I know how awkward and bewildering these encounters can be. This book will help you answer the most common questions Catholics encounter about their faith.

Because I'm not the pope, a bishop, or even a priest, you may be wondering why Liguori Publications asked me to write this book.

I was born and raised in the home of a Protestant pastor in the foothills of North Carolina's Blue Ridge Mountains in 1954. I was a fervent Evangelical Christian. Growing up in the 1950s and 1960s in the midst of the civil rights movement, the Vietnam War, and other societal changes, I found it hard to avoid questions that challenged my childhood faith. I remember the playground debates over electing a Catholic president, and I was able to watch the funeral of Pope John XXIII only because it was a historical event. I firmly believed the pope was the Antichrist and assumed all Catholics were unsaved and destined for hell.

Yet, as a member of a denomination of 40,000, I had an intense curiosity about a Church whose members numbered in the hundreds of millions.

When I attended an Evangelical college, I began losing my connection to my childhood faith, but I knew I couldn't live without "religion" and decided to look at Christianity with fresh eyes.

I began spending Saturdays at a Catholic-college library and went to Saturday-evening Mass out of curiosity. The worship wasn't as beautiful as that of the Episcopal church I usually attended, but it was packed with over 2,000 people—on a Saturday evening. There had to be something to this thing called the Roman Catholic Church.

When I went to an independent Evangelical seminary, Fuller Theological Seminary in Pasadena, California, my interest in Roman Catholicism didn't go away. I met a monk who studied C.S. Lewis, and he invited me to Saint Andrew's Abbey in the Mojave Desert. This experience changed my life. Their way of worship and commitment to God and the Scriptures had a deep sense of purpose. I felt completely drawn to the Catholic tradition, yet it seemed unimaginable to disappoint my parents, relatives, and friends, so I spent years trying to make that tugging feeling go away.

When I began doctoral studies in Reformation history at Cambridge University, my longing to be Catholic became inescapable, and during a weeklong retreat I decided to become Catholic.

The next two years were very painful. My parents expressed fear and hurt, and many friends seemed confused. Most bewildering of all, many Protestant friends and relatives began treating me like a stranger, as though my decision to become Catholic had suddenly made me an alien—someone they had never known. I tried to explain this faith I loved. And while my answers seemed reasonable, those who cornered me remained unconvinced, because their assumptions about Catholicism differed greatly.

My father died in a plane crash three days after I defended my dissertation, but I'm happy to say that we'd had a beautiful reconciliation just weeks earlier. Dad had come to realize that our love for each other was most important and that we could live with our religious differences.

I left Cambridge to teach at the University of Alabama and connected with Saint Francis Parish in Tuscaloosa, where I became involved in Rite of Christian Initiation of Adults (RCIA), wrote prayers for Mass, and enjoyed worship in that lively, dynamic parish.

Yet I found myself dealing with another tug that wouldn't go away. The experience at Saint Andrew's Abbey in the Mojave Desert had made a deep and lasting impression, and I spent five of the most important years of my life as a monk. Living in community, prayerfully reading ancient texts of the faith, and growing in my understanding of Catholic life proved to be a great privilege.

After two years of formation in that desert monastery, I went to Switzerland to complete my theological education at the University of Fribourg. I had the great privilege of working with Father Christoph Schönborn, OP (now Cardinal, Archbishop of Vienna), helping translate drafts of the *Catechism of the Catholic Church.*

After my time in Fribourg, two things became increasingly clear: The priesthood was not my vocation, and I felt most at home in the academic world. In 1992, Saint Louis University invited me to join their faculty.

Saint Louis University is a Catholic university founded by Jesuits, and our department is an ecumenical faculty with a commitment to serve all who study with us. Students must take three theology courses, so professors must articulate valued faith principles in ways that are meaningful to all students.

In addition to my academic work, I have assisted with RCIA instruction at Saint Vincent de Paul Parish near downtown St. Louis, where our catechumens range from the homeless to barely fluent immigrants to corporate executives. Within this parish instruction I have witnessed many people meeting the Church for the first time.

In recent years, my parish has asked me to do monthly question-and-answer sessions at a local microbrewery. The agenda is open and the questions wide-ranging. Folks want direct, honest answers, and that is what I try to give them.

This handbook is in question-and-answer format because that is how you deal with the concerns of those who "corner" you. For them, you are the presence of a Church they find threatening. Follow the lead of the Holy Spirit and avoid responding to their aggressive language with hurtful rebuttals.

When you're asked a question you can't answer, admit it and go find the answer. Always remind questioners that your Catholic faith flows from a desire to grow closer to God, and then reaffirm your willingness to respond to their concerns.

This book is a good place to start looking for answers. The questions here are real, and the answers are straightforward. It's not a catechism, it doesn't condemn other religious traditions—Christian or non-Christian—and it's not the final word on any topic.

I hope and pray that this book supports you in your faith journey and promotes understanding between you and those who question your Catholic faith.

Keep Christ's summary of the law ever before you: Love the Lord God with all your heart, and love your neighbor as yourself. If you're faithful to this Gospel imperative, you'll discover that your ability to provide the "right" answers will be less important than your search to find the fruit of the Holy Spirit in your life.

**Ready Responses
to the Top Five
Questions**

1. Do Catholics believe that non-Catholics can be saved?

The answer: Yes.

During the late 1940s and early 1950s, Boston priest Leonard Feeney, SJ, preached with passion and controversy that there is no salvation outside the Roman Catholic Church. While this teaching was common among Catholics at that time, Cardinal Cushing of Boston recognized that Father Feeney's aggressive and mean-spirited approach offended against the law of charity. Despite Cardinal Cushing's reprimands and orders to stop, Feeney disobeyed his religious superiors and persisted in his preaching. Cardinal Cushing ultimately excommunicated Father Feeney, and the Vatican backed his decision.

At the Second Vatican Council (1962–1965), the bishops prepared a document called In Our Time (*Nostra Aetate*), which clarified that God is present to believers in other Christian traditions, in non-Christian religions, and even in those who are open to the spirit but not connected to a religion. Pope John Paul II famously affirmed this when he gathered 160 world religious leaders (Christian and non-Christian) at Assisi, Italy, in 1986, and they prayed together for peace.

Catholics understand that the love of God is ultimately a mystery and much bigger than human understanding can comprehend (see page 8).

2. Do Catholics worship Mary and the saints?

The answer: No.

Catholics believe the Church is made up of more than the living, breathing Christians you meet on the street, call on the phone, or contact online. Our Christian community includes all who have ever turned their hearts to God and been transformed by God's grace. So Catholics feel comfortable asking Mary—Jesus' mother—and other Christians through the ages to pray for them in times of need, in experiences of joy, and in periods of loneliness.

Catholics don't worship Mary and the saints, but we do admire them in the same way Protestants admire Martin Luther, John Wesley, Dietrich Bonhoeffer, or C.S. Lewis. The great difference is that we believe that our experience of Christian community extends to those who are no longer living and that their prayers can be offered up on our behalf.

This concept was very difficult for my mother to understand until Dad died. She no longer has a problem with the idea of asking Dad to pray for our family and friends and happily reflects on how his prayers have influenced the course of her life and those of her children. For Catholics, the Church is a huge community, and we are encouraged to include the dead in our circle of prayer partners (see pages 57–60).

3. Do Catholics believe the pope is infallible?

The answer: It depends on what you mean by *infallible*.

Catholics believe the Holy Spirit guides the Church and preserves true teaching about our faith. This doesn't mean we believe our leaders are perfect. Our popes are not preserved from sin or miraculously exempt from ordinary human shortcomings. However, Catholics do believe that on extraordinary occasions popes are able to settle points of doctrine that have been debated for centuries. These highly unusual events—so far only two in the history of the Catholic Church—are called *ex cathedra* ("from the chair" of Saint Peter) definitions of doctrine. The First Vatican Council (1869–1870) declared these events to be moments of infallible teaching by popes. This belief flows from our confidence in the Holy Spirit's work in the life of the Church. It is not belief in the man who sits on the chair of Saint Peter (see page 19).

Pope Benedict XVI emphasized this point in his book *Jesus of Nazareth* (Doubleday, 2007): "This book is in no way an exercise of the magisterium, but is solely an expression of my personal search…. Everyone is free, then, to contradict me. I…ask my readers for that initial goodwill without which there can be no understanding."

Due respect and goodwill must always be given to papal teaching, yet we should never forget that the defined limits of papal infallibility are very narrow, and we should use the same caution when talking about it.

FURTHER READING
Christopher Bellitto, *101 Questions and Answers on Popes and the Papacy* (Paulist Press, 2008).

4. Do Catholics believe the Bible is the Word of God?

The answer: The Bible is the Word of God, given for our instruction.

Like our Protestant sisters and brothers, Catholics believe that Jesus is the Word of God made flesh (John 1) and that his presence on Earth continues through the Body of Christ—his Church (1 Corinthians 12:12–28). For this reason, it's not hard for Catholics to accept that the books of the Bible were collected during the first centuries of Christianity and came into existence through the life of the Church.

Today's Bible came together in the fourth and fifth centuries as a definitive collection of sacred texts through the considered opinions of great theologians like Athanasius (293–373) and the decisions of Church councils. It did not come to us whole from heaven, but through human history and through authors inspired by the Holy Spirit. Therefore, we don't separate our reverence of Scripture from our conviction that the Holy Spirit has guided the Church through the centuries. We call this inseparable dimension of God's guiding presence *Tradition* (see pages 83–84).

FURTHER READING

Joseph T. Lienhard, *The Bible, the Church, and Authority: The Canon of the Christian Bible in History and Theology* (Collegeville, MN: Liturgical Press, 1995).

Pontifical Biblical Commission, "The Interpretation of the Bible in the Church" *Origins,* January 6, 1994. catholic-resources.org/ChurchDocs/PBC_Interp.htm.

5. Are Catholics Christian?

The answer: Yes.

Sadly, in the language of American Christianity, too often certain Protestant Christians (often nondenominational) claim the title "Christian" for their understanding of the faith and relegate others—especially Roman Catholics—to a category outside the Christian faith. I've even heard some suggest that Roman Catholicism is a separate religion altogether.

Catholics are Christians, even though the language we use is often different from that of Evangelical Protestants. We don't talk about being "born again"—yet we do understand that our salvation comes through the work of Christ on the cross and the grace given us by the Holy Spirit. We believe our conversion begins at baptism and continues throughout our lives as we grow and mature in our faith.

Protestant Christians rightly want to know how our faith has changed us and what our community is doing to live out the Gospel, so when answering this question I focus on what the Catholic Church does to exemplify the Gospel of Christ rather than pointing out that our Catholic faith stretches back over 2,000 years (see page 12).

Questions About the Institutional Church

Why do Catholics believe they are the only true Church?

This painful issue requires a direct and honest answer. Roman Catholics believe that the Catholic Church has historical continuity with Saint Peter and the apostles who were present on the day of Pentecost, when the Holy Spirit gave birth to the Church. They responded to Jesus' call, found at the end of each of the four Gospels, to go forth and spread the Good News of Christ's resurrection and the coming of the kingdom of God.

Catholics believe that the work begun by Peter and the other apostles continued under men they appointed and on whom they laid hands—giving them "apostolic" authority to carry their work into the next generation. Apostolic authority, understood by Catholics to be historical and traceable, is a mark of authenticity and continuity of the Church. For Catholics, this essential mark of the Church is missing if a Christian community rejects apostolic authority and Peter's leadership of the other apostles—carried on by their successors in the persons of bishops and popes—over the last 2000 years.

This is why, in its 2007 document Responses to Some Questions Regarding Certain Aspects of the Doctrine on the Church, the Congregation for the Doctrine of the Faith stated that Orthodox faith communities are sister Churches. They've maintained their historical continuity with earliest Christianity through the apostolic succession of their bishops. Through their leadership, these Churches maintained a sacramental priesthood that performed eucharistic celebrations that were the heart of early Christian worship. However, because they reject Peter's leadership of the local Churches scattered throughout the world—in the persons of the bishops of Rome—they "suffer from defects."

The case of Christian communities "born out of the Reformation" is more complicated. While these communities rejected the leadership of the bishop of Rome as successor to Saint Peter, some of these Churches (notably the Anglican communion) sought to maintain the historical succession of bishops. The earliest documents of these communities show that they rejected the concept of priesthood as Catholics understand it, meaning they no longer celebrated the Eucharist in an authentic Catholic manner (see page 40). For these reasons, they're described as "ecclesial communities" rather than Churches.

The 2007 document was careful to emphasize that "elements of sanctification and truth" are present in these churches and communities and that "the Spirit of Christ has not refrained from using them as instruments of salvation." Even though these separated Churches and ecclesial communities do not accept elements that Roman Catholics believe are essential for full connection with the earliest Christians, they "are deprived neither of significance nor importance in the mystery of salvation."

Dialogue with other Christians continues, and we hope the love and respect we have for one another can grow over time. Scholars continue to study these questions, and new aspects of significance continue to unfold. While our Church leaders have the role of conserving the faith we have received, all Christians should remember that the Law of Love must prevail. If we violate that principle, we fail to comprehend an essential truth of our faith.

How did Catholics come up with the idea of bishops and priests?

It comes from Scripture and Tradition.

In my childhood denomination, we didn't hold to the lofty title *bishop* for our leaders. We rejected the term *priest* as paganism mixed with true Christian practice. We considered these terms unscriptural additions used by Roman Catholics and Episcopalians. It troubled us that United Methodists and even a few other Holiness churches continued to use the title *bishop* for their leaders.

But it's not that simple. The Greek word for *bishop* (*episkopos*, "supervisor" or "overseer") appears five times in the New Testament. The early German translation of the Greek word *bischof* passed into English—and that is how *bishop* came to be used for the spiritual superintendents of Christian churches.

The English word *priest* comes from the New Testament Greek *presbyteros* ("elder") and suggests a wide range of pastoral responsibilities. It's used to describe Jesus Christ in The Letter to the Hebrews, and all baptized believers are called *priests* in 1 Peter 2:5, 9. The concept of the priesthood of all believers is based on these texts.

By the early second century, those who received the title *episkopos* led the local churches around the Mediterranean. A chief role of these leaders was to preside at the Eucharist, which resembled the Jewish Passover meal commemorating the sacrifice of a spring lamb whose blood was sprinkled on the doorposts of the homes of the Israelites so they would be spared when the angel of death came to kill all the firstborn children in the land. This meal became a Christian celebration of Jesus Christ, the Lamb of God, who cleansed us from the guilt of sin and freed us from the power of sin (spiritual death).

As these Christian communities multiplied and persecution made it impossible for the bishop to be present to all the believers of a local church, the work of celebrating the Eucharist was delegated to the elder (priest). By the end of the second century, the eucharistic leadership of bishops and priests in worship defined their roles within the local church.

Far from being "unbiblical" additions to Christian teaching, bishops and priests helped connect long-standing Jewish practice with the faith Jesus introduced. This connection with the Passover meal created a unique bond between God and the Christian community as the Lamb of God became a meal for the faithful, where together we celebrate the forgiveness of sins and fellowship with God, gain strength for the journey through our spiritual deserts, and lead us to our intended destination—the kingdom of God.

Why do Catholics think the Church is part of the Gospel? Isn't faith in the Gospel of Jesus fundamental?

Catholics celebrate Pentecost as the birthday of the Church. In Acts of the Apostles 2:1–41, the Holy Spirit descends on the disciples fifty days after Jesus' resurrection and fills them with grace and the authority to proclaim the Good News about Jesus. Led by Saint Peter, Christians started in Jerusalem and then traveled throughout the Roman Empire and beyond, calling others to the saving knowledge of Jesus Christ.

Fundamentally, Roman Catholics believe the Holy Spirit works through the Church—the Body of Christ—to be Christ's presence in the world. The Vatican II document Dogmatic Constitution on the Church (*Lumen Gentium*) called the Church the "People of God" (16) and a "spiritual community" (8). Catholics believe that we cannot be Christians by ourselves. Faith in Jesus necessarily means that we belong to a community. That is what we mean by "Church."

The New Testament contains different models for organizing Christian communities, but common elements have endured: faith in Jesus as the Messiah and Christ, the practice of baptizing new members and celebrating the Eucharist (what many Protestants call the Lord's Supper), the expectation that Christ will come again to establish the kingdom of God on Earth, and the obligation to preach, instruct, and love one another. These are all elements in the Roman Catholic understanding of "Church."

In the New Testament, the local churches in diverse places—and the whole Church throughout the world—are the means by which the Holy Spirit works in the world. In Saint Paul's pastoral letters (1 and 2 Timothy and Titus), leaders of the Church received their authority from Jesus' apostles—what Catholics call *apostolic au-*

thority (see pages 8 and 9). These leaders had instructions to teach, provide pastoral care to, and organize the Christian community. These themes are reinforced in Acts. When necessary, these leaders exercised discipline and corrected members of the Christian community—the Church. These institutional structures of Roman Catholicism are drawn from the Bible.

Many Protestant churches and independent Christian fellowships may claim there is no warrant for the Roman Catholic Church—as Church—in Scripture, but our Church is grounded in biblical teaching. The evidence is overwhelming.

FURTHER READING

Avery Cardinal Dulles, SJ, *Models of the Church* (1974; 1987 revision published by Image Books).

How can a Christian live under leaders who are treated like they are beyond the spiritual level of the laity?

There is temptation in every Christian tradition to place leaders on a pedestal—beyond the laity. This has happened with televangelists, pastors of megachurches, and preachers in small storefront congregations, too often with tragic consequences as personal failings and concealed sins come to public attention and destroy communities that had placed their trust more in their leadership than in God's grace.

Roman Catholics aren't immune from this temptation. Some Catholics—even Catholic leaders—like to think our clergy are immune from human weakness or that Catholic ordination supernaturally preserves clergy from poor judgment and human error.

But this isn't what Catholic Tradition teaches about Church leadership. Deacons, priests, bishops, and the pope are all men in need of God's grace, men who must regularly examine their actions and decisions, confess their sins and failures, and seek reconciliation just like all other believers.

What Catholics do believe is that even a priest, bishop, or pope in a state of sin can be an agent through whom God's grace can be communicated to the faithful. This is jarring for some Protestants. But through the sacraments—especially the Eucharist, reconciliation, and the anointing of the sick—these men have the opportunity to touch the lives of laypeople and communicate God's love in tangible and reassuring ways.

This work must never be understood as power over the laity. It's a sacred trust and duty. If you encounter an ordained man who has forgotten that his work is to serve, search for one who understands that ordination confers *servanthood*—not power.

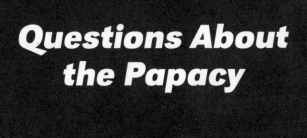

Why do Catholics call the pope, rather than Christ, the head of the Church?

Catholics believe that the Church is the Body of Christ and that Christ is the head of the Church. Gleaned from Scripture (Ephesians 1:22 and 5:23; Colossians 1:18), this is a biblical conclusion on which all Christians agree.

Where Protestants, Orthodox believers, and Catholics part company is the role of the bishop of Rome as the leader of the Church on Earth. Catholic apologists point to Matthew 16:18 and John 21:15–17 as evidence that Christ made Peter's faith the foundation of the Church and appointed him to care for his flock and lead the bishops. These interpretations have been a source of controversy not only between Catholics and non-Catholics, but also among Catholics.

Yet in recent decades, major Protestant biblical scholars have come to agree that Peter—not simply Peter's faith in Jesus—is the rock referenced in Matthew. John 21 proves more problematic for Catholic apologists. Raymond Brown, Pope Paul VI's biblical theologian, emphasized that the sheep belong to Christ, not to Peter.

The concept of vicar (overseer) of Christ dates back at least to the late first or early second century. Saint Ignatius introduced the idea in his epistle to the Magnesians when he stated, "Your bishop presides in the place of God." The Vatican II document *Lumen Gentium* teaches that all bishops are vicars of Christ (27).

But the term began to be used for the bishop of Rome as early as the fifth century, when it was used to describe Pope Gelasius' pastoral role as the vicar and pastor who would feed Christ's flock (the Church) in place of Christ (associated with John 21). It became commonly used by western Christians in the 1200s.

While Catholics do place their faith in Christ as the head of the Church, they look to the pope for earthly leadership and guidance. This ancient practice reinforces the sense of continuity in the life of the Church and reassures us that while Christ hasn't yet returned, he hasn't left us without a leader and guide.

Though Catholics know that popes are not perfect men, we trust that the Holy Spirit guides the Church and that God's truth will prevail even when papal leadership is less than perfect.

FURTHER READING

Raymond Brown, *The Churches the Apostles Left Behind,* Paulist Press, 1984.

How can you trust the papacy when it has such a checkered past?

When I was about nine, I discovered a Western Civilization textbook that outlined the horrors of the medieval papacy and Reformation-era Catholicism, the Crusades, the Borgia popes, the Inquisition, the selling of indulgences, the Protestant martyrdoms in Mary Tudor's England, and the treachery of the Saint Bartholomew's Day massacre in France. I couldn't imagine how anyone could be Catholic.

But years later, as a serious student of Reformation history, I came to realize that no Church has been spared the human failings of its leaders or followers. The abuses first-generation Protestant reformers had sought to correct seemed to return in the practice of second- and third-generation Protestants. While Mary Tudor's misdeeds had been chronicled in John Foxe's sixteenth-century book *Acts and Monuments,* Queen Elizabeth had been equally ruthless toward Catholics. Like all humans, all Christian Churches and communities "have sinned and are deprived of the glory of God" (Romans 3:23). This significant hurdle needed to be jumped, not tiptoed around.

Once I understood this truth, it was possible to look at the good that could be found in the history of the papacy and the Catholic Church and its positive impact in the midst of human limitations and failings. These became, in a significant way, markers of the Holy Spirit at work in the life of the Catholic Church.

How did the idea of papal infallibility come about?

Papal infallibility is one of the most misunderstood aspects of Roman Catholicism—both inside and outside the Catholic Church. The confusion results from an internal debate that stretches back over hundreds of years and has been resolved in different directions by Church councils.

Debates over papal authority and the authority of bishops were complicated, because Catholic theologians and Church leaders didn't want to feed Protestants' hatred of the papacy. Often those who sought dialogue with Protestants emphasized the Church's government as representative, stressed the collective role of bishops, and downplayed the ultimate authority of popes. Others described the papacy as a type of monarchy and argued that popes had absolute and unrestricted powers.

In the early 1800s, both theories of authority had strong representation in different parts of the Catholic world. Many treated this difference as an honest disagreement that could be tolerated within the Church. Yet by the mid-nineteenth century, Pope Pius IX and important Church leaders pressed for a resolution of this question.

The First Vatican Council, which met in 1869–1870, proved a very contentious doctrinal event. While the majority of bishops at the council came from regions that favored strong papal authority, a large minority of bishops represented those who gave greater weight to the involvement of bishops when settling doctrinal questions and disputed Church affairs. The argument boiled down to the following question: Is the pope's infallible authority personal (belonging to the man in office), absolute (with no restriction on how and when it is used), and separate (not accountable to or limited by the bishops in any way)?

The resulting document, *Pastor Aeternus,* made it clear that infallible papal authority belongs to the office, not the man. The man remains fallible and human in every way. The pope has infallible authority only when he states explicitly that he is speaking *ex cathedra* ("from the chair" of Saint Peter as head of the Church on Earth). Finally, the document stated that this infallible authority does not depend on the approval of the other bishops of the Church.

Since that document was issued, infallible authority has been exercised only once, when Pius XII defined the dogma of Mary's assumption into heaven in 1950. (Pope Pius IX defined the dogma of the Immaculate Conception in 1854, before Vatican I.) Yet it is important to note that while he settled this theological question without calling a council, Pius XII did consult bishops around the world. Ninety-eight percent of them agreed with his conclusions and affirmed that it was a good time to settle the question.

Papal infallibility remains a controversial question both inside and outside the Church. However, three things should be made clear: first, infallible papal authority does not mean that the man who holds the office has ceased to be a fallible human being; second, this authority is rarely used; and third, while it can be exercised without consulting brother bishops, this has never happened, and with good reason: Catholics believe the Holy Spirit guides and directs the Church in the ways of truth, and the guidance of the Holy Spirit is best discerned when the whole body of Christ—the Church on Earth—is engaged in understanding the signs of the times and the needs of Christians.

Questions About
the Priesthood

Who can be a priest?

According to the Catholic Church's *Code of Canon Law* (1024), only a baptized man can be considered for priestly ordination. Beyond this basic requirement, it becomes more complicated. Ordinarily, candidates in the Roman Rite must be celibate, unmarried men (see page 24). However, Pope John Paul II began making exceptions in cases of married Anglican and Lutheran clergymen who became Catholics and sought ordination in the Roman Catholic Church.

The Eastern Rite Churches, in communion with Rome, ordain celibate and married men.

Women are not permitted to seek priestly ordination (see page 25).

What do Catholics believe about "the priesthood of all believers"?

Following the biblical principles set out in 1 Peter 2:4–12 (which mirrors Exodus 19:5–6), the documents of Vatican II emphasize that all the baptized are a "body of priests" called to offer their lives as a spiritual sacrifice pleasing to God.

As a whole, the priesthood of all believers shares in the three-fold mission of Christ, who is prophet, priest, and king. Catholics believe that the ordained priesthood can be properly understood only within this context.

The laity and the ordained priesthood share a common dignity, grace, and vocation to seek perfection according to their own calling. Yet they have different functions in the Church, as Paul emphasized in 1 Corinthians 12:12–28 and as the council fathers explained at Vatican II in the 1965 document Decree on the Apostolate of the Laity (*Apostolicam Actuositatem*, 3).

Why are most Roman Catholic priests unmarried?

Scriptural evidence supports the idea that bishops, presbyters, and deacons should be "married only once" (1 Timothy 3:2, 12). The biblical basis for celibate priests is found in 1 Corinthians 7:1, 7. While critics point out that other portions of 1 Corinthians 7 indicate that celibacy should be optional, from the early centuries of Christianity, celibacy has been encouraged as a way for priests to follow the example of Christ.

Yet in the Greek- and Latin-speaking Churches, this discipline remained optional for diocesan clergy during the first thousand years of Christianity. The Orthodox Churches still allow their parish priests to marry, though their bishops must be celibate men (they usually come from monastic communities).

The Roman rite Catholic Church's celibate priesthood is often attributed to the medieval Church's application of monastic discipline to diocesan priests. This tendency stretched over centuries. Yet the requirement of celibacy for all Roman rite clergy became Pope Gregory VII's chief tool to end the widespread scandal of *simony* (clergy selling Church property for personal gain) and *nepotism* (clergy placing their children in Church offices and transferring Church property to them) in the 1070s.

As the number of priests declines, changes to this discipline have been urged even by senior cardinals. Although Pope John Paul II made exceptions with the ordination of married Anglican and Lutheran clergymen who become Catholics, he also strongly defended the celibate clergy in his "Theology of the Body" instructions.

FURTHER READING

Helen Parish, *Clerical Celibacy in the West: c.1100–1700* (Ashgate, 2010).

Why can't women be ordained to the priesthood?

The official reason is that Jesus appointed only men to be his apostles, and the Church is following his example. In his 1994 apostolic letter On Reserving Priestly Ordination to Men Alone (*Ordinatio Sacerdotalis*), Pope John Paul II stated emphatically that he lacked the authority to alter this practice, since he judged this to be the practice of the Church from the beginning. This continues to be the position of Benedict XVI and other Church leaders.

Until recently, almost all Christian churches—including ecclesial communities that don't consider their clergy to be a sacrificial priesthood—didn't ordain women. In the mid 1800s, the American Holiness denominations were the earliest to ordain women (Quaker and early Methodist women preached and were leaders, but they were not ordained). Yet even in the Holiness tradition, the ordination of women became rare by the early 1900s. Movements for the ordination of women in the Anglican communion and other Protestant denominations began to gain momentum by the middle of the twentieth century, and since the early 1960s many—but not all—Protestant denominations have begun ordaining women.

Until the early 1970s, little scholarly work had been devoted to the history of women within the Christian tradition, and almost no research was devoted to the history of women in ministry. While in recent decades scholars have traced evidence of the priestly ordination of women in the early Church, this scholarship hasn't gained widespread acceptance among Christian communities that don't ordain women.

It shouldn't surprise us that Roman Catholic leaders are cautious in their judgments. They see their role as conservers of the faith received and are reluctant to accept arguments suggesting that an ancient practice has lain dormant for over 1800 years. This reluctance has intensified because the new evidence has emerged in a period when women's roles in Western culture have radically changed.

It's important to note that even though John Paul's apostolic letter was strongly worded and Cardinal Avery Dulles said the letter amounted to an infallible statement, the pope did not declare his judgment *ex cathedra*. Time will tell whether a future pope or council, after examining the growing body of historical evidence, will come to a different judgment.

Questions About Monasticism and Vocational Life

What is the role of monasticism in the Catholic Church?

Monks and nuns are men and women who dedicate their lives to praying, building Christian community, and sharing the fruits of their labors. They believe in the power of prayer, gathering several times a day (generally three to seven times) to pray, read Scripture, and reflect on God's presence in the world. Often they practice forms of prayer that engage their thoughts as they work.

Monasticism became a rapidly growing aspect of Christian life by the late 200s in Syria and Egypt. Some historians observe that when Constantine made Christianity the official religion of the Roman Empire in the early 300s, Christians who wanted to demonstrate their devotion and to live heroically left the comforts of cities and villages to live in the desert. Some of these early Egyptian monastic leaders, like Saint Anthony the Great (251–356), lived alone as eremites (religious hermits). Others gathered in communities, sharing everything and living under the authority of an abbot (or spiritual father). The reputed founder of monasticism in Europe was Saint Benedict of Nursia (480–543). Benedict's *Rule* became the standard handbook for how a monastic community should regulate its life.

Monasticism was important in the first thousand years of Christianity because of its pioneering and missionary-minded spirit. Monasteries established points of stability and Christian formation in regions not yet touched by Christianity. This witness to the faith resulted in the spread of Christianity throughout Europe. Prior to the 1500s, monks and nuns were perhaps the most effective missionaries in the history of Christianity. Today they continue to be missionaries, establishing monasteries and converting others to the faith by their example and teaching.

Are Catholic religious orders dying?

Almost all western European and North American religious orders have experienced a significant decline in their numbers. Some reasons for this are cultural and some result from the changing views of how Catholics can live out their faith. One often hears that young people aren't convinced they have to be celibate to live a life focused on Gospel principles.

As a professor at a Catholic Jesuit university, I am inspired by young people and sense that this decline in vocations is not a decline in serious Christian living.

Other parts of the world are not experiencing this decline. In Africa, Latin America, and Asia, religious orders and priestly vocations are growing significantly.

We're living in a period of change. As the majority of Catholics now live in the southern hemisphere, perhaps this is as it should be.

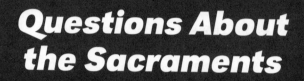

Questions About the Sacraments

What do Catholics mean when they talk about sacraments?

Catholics believe that the incarnation of Jesus Christ is the first sacrament, for he is the Word made flesh and the ultimate manifestation of God's power and love (grace) in time and space. The Church too is a sacrament, for it is the Body of Christ and the ongoing earthly manifestation of God's power and love in time and space.

All sacramental manifestations of God's love and power proceed through Christ's passion, death, and resurrection. This is referred to as a "mystery," or as the early Greek-speaking Christians called it, *mysterion*. The use of this term emphasized the "hidden" nature of God's plan that became known in human history to those who believe (Matthew 13:11; Romans 16:25–26; Ephesians 1:9–10).

Roman Catholics experience this grace through seven liturgical rites called *sacraments*, yet the *mysterion* is broader and richer than these seven rites. Any earthly manifestation of God's love and power is a sacramental experience.

Around the 200s, Tertullian translated the Greek word *mysterion* into the Latin term *sacramentum*, which means "oath" or "pledge," a word used for the initiation of soldiers in the Roman military. When a soldier made his oath/pledge, his arm was branded with the name of the general he served. Tertullian used the word *sacramentum* to explain that baptism is the permanent consecration of the believer to God's service. Just as the soldier's pledge was made through word (the oath) and visible sign (brand), so too the believer is consecrated to God through word (the baptismal rite) and visible sign (water).

Saint Augustine (354–430) took up this understanding of the *mysterion/sacramentum*, emphasizing that sacraments are signs of God's love and power (grace). These signs have two key elements: words and material elements. As generations of Christians reflected

31

on this mystery, these two dimensions proved an important way to talk about the sacramental rites of the Church.

From the 1000s to the 1200s, western Christians identified seven sacraments administered by the Church and used by God to sanctify humanity and unite the Body of Christ: baptism, confirmation, Eucharist, reconciliation (or penance, also called confession), anointing of the sick, marriage, and holy orders.

While these seven sacraments are understood to be "instrumental causes" of grace—outward signs instituted by Christ to give grace—Catholics understand that the mystery of God's love and power in the world are not limited to these liturgical rites in the Catholic Church. Wherever we find the grace unleashed by Christ's passion, death, and resurrection manifested in the world, God is sacramentally present. It is ultimately a mystery (*mysterion*).

Do Catholics believe non-Catholic baptisms are valid?

A person can be validly baptized only once, whether in or out of the Catholic Church. Catholics believe three things are necessary for a valid baptism:

- use of the Trinitarian formula (baptizing in the name of the Father, and the Son, and the Holy Spirit),

- flowing water (immersing, pouring, or sprinkling on the forehead), and

- the intention of the "minister" to baptize the person using the form (words of the Trinitarian formula) and matter (flowing water) needed for a valid baptism.

Baptisms in the Catholic Church are normally performed by priests or deacons. But in unusual circumstances, especially when there is danger of death, any person can be a valid "minister" of this sacrament, even a non-Christian who has the right intention, because God—not the person performing the baptism—is giving us grace.

Orthodox and most Protestant baptisms conform to these expectations and are recognized by the Catholic Church. However, baptisms performed by Christian communities that don't believe in the Trinity aren't recognized as valid. These communities include Jehovah's Witnesses, Jesus-Only Pentecostals (also called Oneness Pentecostals), and One-God Holiness groups as well as Mormons, who don't understand the Trinity in the same way as Catholic, Orthodox, and most Protestant believers. They may use the same matter (flowing water), but they don't have the same form (Trinitarian formula) or intention in their baptism.

Why are you Catholic?

This question must be answered out of your own experience, but here are a few observations and suggestions.

Cradle Catholics

If you were born and baptized Catholic in infancy, you may think that's your answer. However, some people ask this question to challenge your faith, asking if you're "born again" or have a "personal relationship with Jesus Christ." This isn't language familiar to many Catholics, so you may be confused over how to answer the question. Non-Catholics may see that confusion as uncertainty and a reason to try to convert you to another way of living the Christian faith.

The plain truth is that through the sacraments of baptism and confirmation, you *have* been "born again," and through the sacraments of the Eucharist and reconciliation—as well as prayer and fellowship in your parish—your personal relationship with Jesus Christ *is* continually deepening. Therefore, the answer to both questions is yes.

If you're unsettled by the question posed by those who seek to convert you to their practice of the faith, talk to a priest or trusted Catholic lay leader in your parish.

Adults who become Catholic

The reasons adults become Catholic can range widely. For me, it was a strong sense that the Catholic tradition had a breadth and depth of spiritual practices that my childhood denomination didn't. The resources to grow in my Christian life through the many different ways to be Catholic proved the strongest reasons for my decision to seek reception into the Roman Catholic Church.

You may have had a profound experience in one of the sacraments or devotional practices of the Catholic Church. A "mystical" moment may have confirmed for you that this was the right decision for your life.

For others, this decision is bound up with personal relationships. A fiancé(e), spouse, relatives, friends, an impressive priest or person in religious life, or a positive experience with a Catholic group or Catholic colleagues are important starting points and reasonable responses to questions about why you are Catholic. Obviously, you want to go deeper and understand how the Catholic experience of faith can draw you into a deeper knowledge of God's presence in your life. By reading this book, you're doing just that.

A word about the word *conversion*

In Christianity, conversion is to faith in Jesus Christ, not to a religious tradition. Many—perhaps most—adults who become Roman Catholic already have received baptism and been formed in another Christian tradition. To call these persons "converts" is a misnomer in the strict sense of the term, although I've often used it as shorthand for my own experience.

I experienced conversion through faith in Jesus Christ and the grace of baptism as a Protestant. I grew into a deeper understanding of that conversion as I came to know and love the Roman Catholic Church. Because Catholics understand conversion to be a daily, ongoing process, it's reasonable to say I'm a convert. But that's describing my daily experience of faith, not my change of Church membership.

Are you going to try to convert me to Catholicism?

Friends and relatives often fear your relationship has changed. They worry that you'll make "being like you" the new standard for that relationship. I always find it best to reassure those I care about, reminding them that I respect them and that this decision has been important in *my* life. I'm not making a decision for *them*.

If they're living a fervent Christian life in another tradition, speak positively about their experience and be genuine about your respect for their faith life. Ask for the same respect in return. If it isn't given, live by example.

Does the person who asks this question live a life that is destructive of faith? If so, they may want you to continue joining them in activities and behaviors that will draw you away from your Catholic faith. Always be respectful, but make it clear that your life has changed and that some things are in the past for you. Through the witness of your changed life, you may well end up converting that person, and that can only be a good thing.

Why do Catholics think the Eucharist is a sacrifice?

Because the Eucharist has its origins in a Jewish sacrificial rite—the Passover—earliest Christians understood it to be a "sacrifice." That belief continues among Roman Catholics, Orthodox Christians, and some Anglicans. At Jesus' final Passover meal—which Christians commonly call the Last Supper—he identified with the sacrificed lamb at the center of that shared religious meal. As Jesus blessed and distributed the bread and wine, he described them as his Body and Blood and admonished his disciples to eat and drink these. He called the bread "my body, which will be given for you" (Luke 22:19). He explained that the wine is "my blood of the covenant" (Matthew 26:28; Mark 14:24; Luke 22:20). He urged the disciples to continue this practice "in memory of me" (Luke 22:19).

In these Gospel texts, Jesus placed the Jewish communion sacrifice of Passover in a new context. While it remained a religious meal shared figuratively with God and literally with those present, it also established a new covenant relationship. Jesus became the Lamb sacrificed and shared. Yet, more important, his self-giving became the center of the celebration and the mark of unity between God and the gathered community.

Catholics believe the Eucharist is a sacrifice as well as a celebration and an experience of joy. Jesus reconciled us and renewed our covenant relationship with God. That is why we come together to experience anew the moment when our guilt was removed and God's love for us affirmed. The Eucharist remains a ready, tangible reminder of our fellowship with other Christians and God. This is experienced through the consecrated bread and wine, which in the mystery of God's love becomes for us the Body and Blood of Christ.

What do Catholics mean by *transubstantiation*?

How can one describe a mystery in human language? In the 1100s this became a challenge as theologians argued about what happened during the consecration of the bread and wine at the Eucharist. Some theologians maintained that the elements—bread and wine—were mere *signs* of Christ's Body and Blood. Others argued that the elements *became* the physical components of Jesus' earthly body.

Theologians in western Europe were fascinated by the Greek philosopher Aristotle's distinction between the changeable accidents of an object (its texture, color, taste—elements that are perceptible to human senses) and the object's substance (its pure existence apart from accidents the senses can perceive).

Theologians in the 1100s and 1200s came to talk about the mystery of Christ's presence in the Eucharist as *transubstantiation*, a theological term coined to explain the paradox of the changeable accidents of bread and wine remaining unaltered to the human senses, while the substance (pure existence) of the bread and wine was transformed into the Body and Blood of Christ.

This use of newly recovered Aristotelian language to explain a central mystery of the Christian faith proved a great aid in settling the debates among theologians in this period. The term *transubstantiation* became a part of western Christian theology because the Second Lateran Council (1215) used it to explain this mystery. Catholic reflections and devotions—focused on the Eucharist—became deeply influenced by this Aristotelian distinction.

During Vatican II (1962–1965), the bishops and Pope Paul VI discussed dropping the term *transubstantiation* from the Catholic vocabulary because Aristotelian language no longer adequately explained this mystery in the twentieth century. In the end, the term was retained, but the pope and bishops recognized that our understanding of the term must be influenced by the philosophical language of this era. Pope Paul VI explained the importance of this shifting understanding in his 1965 encyclical on the Eucharist, The Mystery of Faith (*Mysterium Fidei*).

No human language ever adequately explains how a mystery like Christ's presence in the Eucharist can happen. As long as we keep this in mind, the debates over terms and what they attempt to describe can be seen for what they are: feeble human efforts to explain mystery. God's reality is much bigger than our efforts to put it into words.

Why are non-Catholics not allowed to receive Communion at Catholic Masses?

This painful question often arises at times when symbols of unity are most eagerly desired. Baptisms, weddings, funerals, and other crucial moments bring family and friends from diverse backgrounds together. On these occasions it seems harsh to remind each other of our lack of unity on crucial matters of faith.

Catholics understand the Eucharist to be a paschal sacrifice that celebrates the covenant between God and believers who share unity of faith and practice. Because this sacrament is an outward sign of spiritual unity between God and fellow Christians, reception of the Eucharist is restricted to baptized Catholics in good standing with the Church. The Catholic Church is not the only ecclesial community to do this, but it is the most prominent.

Canon law identifies lack of unity as the barrier to intercommunion. These barriers include not being baptized, making life choices that transgress Church discipline, not believing in Christ's presence in the Eucharist, and refusing to accept Catholic Church leadership (priests who offer sacrificial service at the Eucharist, bishops who stand in apostolic succession, and the bishop of Rome as the head of the Church). These are all understood to be signs of our unity of faith and practice.

It should be noted that canon 844, which outlines the ordinary practice of the Church, has several key exceptions. Even though Eastern Orthodox Christians and some other ecclesial communities reject the leadership of the bishop of Rome, they do have apostolic leadership and a belief in the sacraments that parallel Roman Catholic beliefs. Therefore, they are allowed to receive Communion at Catholic Masses. Permission can also be arranged for Christians from other ecclesial communities if they meet three criteria: 1) they are cut off from the ministry of their own clergy, 2) they request access to Roman Catholic sacraments, and 3) they profess beliefs that are parallel to those of Catholics.

The presumption of the priest should always be charitable, so it is rare for a priest to judge the spiritual state of any person who comes to Communion. The responsibility rests with the individual who comes to receive the sacrament. When Communion is restricted, the priest is obligated to explain why.

Why isn't the chalice always offered with the Eucharist?

The simple answer is that Catholics consider Communion to be whole and complete whether a communicant receives the consecrated bread, consecrated wine, or both.

Before Vatican II (1962–1965), the chalice was forbidden to the laity and reserved for the presiding priest. When the emphasis of the liturgy shifted to focus on the paschal sacrifice—the shared meal—receiving both not only became permitted, but the preferred way of receiving Communion (see page 37). However, there remain circumstances—for example, at Masses where thousands are present—when the presiding priest(s) may offer only the consecrated host to the laity.

Why must Catholics confess their sins to a priest?

The sacrament of reconciliation (also called penance or confession), like the other sacraments Catholics cherish, is an experience of God's love and power in the world (grace). The believer is touched and healed by God's presence through outward signs of matter (in this case, the physical presence of a priest) and form (the words of the rite of penance). The real question about reconciliation is not why one *has* to do this, but why a person wouldn't *want* to experience God's grace in this way.

Early Christians recognized that forgiveness for postbaptismal sins required a special experience of reconciliation. The early forms of this sacrament were rigorous and offered by the Church only once in a person's life. But Irish Christians introduced a more compassionate form of reconciliation that involved private confession to a priest, and they urged Christians to use the sacrament often. This became the common practice of western Christians until the 1500s, when some Protestant reformers questioned the practice of confession altogether. They argued that there was no need for a priest, since one could receive forgiveness of sins directly through Christ.

These reformers failed to appreciate the human need to receive reassurance of forgiveness of sins that comes from the sacramental encounter with a priest. What we are often unable to accept or believe through our private prayers, a priest can confirm as a representative of Christ's presence in the world. As with the other sacraments, this is not something God requires before forgiving, but a means by which we can hear and believe that God's love really does extend to us even in the midst of our sins and failures to live by God's principles.

Today most Catholics use the prayer at the beginning of Mass to seek forgiveness for the small ways in which we have failed to live by God's principles and broken fellowship with our community. In recent decades, many Catholics seek reconciliation only when they have major crises or significant lapses in their life of faith. This is a very different approach to the pre-Vatican II experience of older Catholics, who remember going to confession on Saturday as a necessary step before receiving Communion at Mass on Sunday. As a minimum requirement, Catholics are expected to confess grave sins once a year through the sacrament of reconciliation (Code of Canon Law, 989). However, the Church recommends that Catholics seek Christ in the sacrament of reconciliation more often, because the benefits in grace and peace are so positive.

So while Catholics do not believe they must confess *every* sin to a priest, the sacrament of reconciliation is a time when we can seek assurance of God's love even as we grieve over the ways we have sinned and hurt others. Hearing the words of the priest and receiving a blessing at his hands provides us with tangible reminders of God love and capacity to see beyond our failings and love us as we seek to mend the harm we have inflicted on others.

What do Catholics mean by "sacramental marriage"?

Marriage, like other sacraments, is a way to experience God's love and power (grace) in the world. In the history of the Church, a developing understanding of sacraments emerged over time. It wasn't until the twelfth century that marriage came to be expressed in the way we express the ritual today, but there had long been a belief in the sanctity of the sacramental bond. Traditionally treated as a legal "contract," the sacrament of marriage since Vatican II (1962–1965) has been explored using the term covenant as the most appropriate theological language for the relationship between spouses.

The word *covenant* brings to mind God's covenant relationship with the people of Israel and Christ's relationship with the Church. This is neither accident nor analogy. Those who covenant themselves in a sacramental marriage understand that they are the ministers of God's love and power to their spouse. Because this sacramental life is an eternal religious reality witnessed by God, only adults who are mentally, emotionally, and spiritually mature can make such a sacred commitment.

Marriage is sometimes viewed as a contract entered into for the good of society but which can be severed, but the Church teaches differently. God creates an unbreakable sacramental bond when a man and woman understand the meaning of that covenant relationship, have no psychological impediments to making the commitment, and are spiritually prepared to enter this sacramental way of life.

While the marriage bond expresses love and commitment between spouses, it also represents the mutual love and shared life between God and God's people and between Christ and the Church. This is a sacramental ministry from which the love and power of God can be poured out into the world.

Questions About Worship

Given what Jesus says in Matthew 18:20, why must a priest preside at Mass?

This text from Matthew—"where two or three are gathered together in my name, there am I in the midst of them"—is undoubtedly true. However, while it speaks to the experience of believers gathered in prayer, it doesn't follow that this passage applies to eucharistic celebrations. In that matter, Catholics have almost 2,000 years of precedent to consider.

Since the earliest period of the Church, Christians have been led in eucharistic celebration by bishops and the priests they delegate (see page 10). Catholic eucharistic liturgies are based on this hierarchical structure. Of the many traditions cherished by Catholics, this is among the oldest historically verifiable practices of the Church.

Why do Catholics *have* to go to Mass *every week?*

Catholics are expected to attend Mass each week not because the Church makes onerous rules, but because the Ten Commandments expressly states that one day in seven should be a time of rest and worship. The importance of the Sabbath precept (counted as the third commandment by Catholics and the fourth commandment by Protestants) makes this a serious matter.

The original Jewish practice began at sunset the evening before. This is still Jewish practice. Early Christians transferred the day of worship and rest from the last day of the week (Saturday) to the first day of the week (Sunday) in honor of the day of Christ's resurrection. This is why Christians commonly refer to Sunday as the "Lord's Day."

I've sometimes heard Protestants imply that Catholics cheat by attending a Saturday evening Mass instead of a Sunday Mass. However, this custom follows the older Jewish practice of reckoning the Sabbath and other holy days from sunset the day before. A Saturday vigil Mass is part of the Sunday celebration.

What are holy days, and why do Catholics celebrate them?

For most of the history of Christianity, the vast majority of Christians couldn't read. They learned about sacred events and holy people through images (see page 62) and rituals that helped them understand Christian life. Holy days gave the faithful time away from their ordinary work to reflect on these things. Before the notion of vacations, holy days created times of rest and refreshment from the monotony of daily life. They also contributed to the growth of community life through shared celebration.

Today, however, vacations help us escape from our routines, so holy days focus on faith. The liturgical calendar lists many feasts, solemnities, and memorials, but the Church considers particular holy days that pertain to Catholic identity to be important opportunities for spiritual growth. The holy days of obligation vary by country and diocese, but in general, United States Catholics are expected to attend Mass on the following days as well as Sundays: Mary the Mother of God (January 1), Ascension (sixth Thursday or the sixth Sunday after Easter), Assumption (August 15), All Saints (November 1), Immaculate Conception (December 8), and Christmas (December 25).

In Hawaii, Christmas and the Immaculate Conception are the only holy days of obligation.

Why do Catholics make the Sign of the Cross?

This gesture has been a Christian practice for at least 1800 years. In the earliest period, it was a way to greet other believers during periods of persecution and to bless every activity of life. Tertullian (c.155–after 220) described it as a simple tracing of the cross on one's forehead. This became the gesture priests used in blessing people, and parents came to use it when blessing their children.

Later Christians added another form, moving the right hand from the forehead to the breast, and then from the left shoulder to the right shoulder. The movement from forehead to breast symbolized Christ's descent from glory to dwell with us on Earth, and the gesture from left to right symbolized Christ's crossing from death to new life.

Even the way Christians held their fingers had theological significance. During an early Christian controversy, two fingers were used to remind believers that Christ had two natures (human and divine). In another period, three fingers invoked the Holy Trinity. An open hand also came to be used by some, with the five fingers understood to represent the five wounds of Jesus on the cross.

When the Gospel is about to be read, Catholics trace a cross on their forehead, lips, and breast. This form represents a prayer some Catholics also say to themselves: "May Christ's words be in my mind, on my lips, and in my heart."

This gesture is filled with meaning and significance for Catholics. It is a powerful reminder of Christ's work on the cross and of how we are bound to him through grace.

FURTHER READING
Andreas Andreopoulos, *The Sign of the Cross* (Paraclete Press, 2006).

What is holy water?

Holy water is ordinary water that has been blessed by a priest. Its primary purpose is to remind us of the waters of baptism and of the grace that comes to us through baptism.

Holy water is usually placed in a font near the entrance of a church or chapel. Worshipers dip the fingers of their right hand in the font before making the Sign of the Cross. This practice may go all the way back to Roman times, where the basilicas of Rome usually had fountains where worshipers could wash their hands and faces before services.

Priests will sometimes sprinkle the congregation with holy water during services as a reminder of the waters of baptism.

Why does a lamp burn in Catholic churches?

The sanctuary lamp came into the Christian tradition through Jewish temple practice. Exodus 27:20–21 says that a lamp must be perpetually lit outside the Holy of Holies, where the ark was kept and the presence of God was manifest. Jewish synagogues still maintain an eternal flame in front of the place where the Torah (God's Word) is kept.

Catholics maintain this practice by keeping a lamp lit before the *tabernacle* (a term borrowed from the Jewish temple tradition), the place where the "Word made flesh" present in the consecrated eucharistic bread is "reserved."

Why do Catholics stop to kneel on one knee as they move from one part of a church to another?

This gesture is called *genuflection*. Catholics do this just before we enter the pew, as we leave the pew, and when we pass before the tabernacle—the place where the consecrated bread is kept. This act of reverence before the Blessed Sacrament is a reminder of God's presence in the tabernacle.

Catholics who are physically unable to genuflect can bow at the waist instead.

Why do Catholics use incense in their worship?

Jewish temple practice and pagan worship in the first century used incense in their liturgies. Luke 1:10 reported its use in Jewish worship (also see Leviticus 6:15 and 1 Chronicles 9:29). The psalmist wrote, "Let my prayer be incense before you; my uplifted hands an evening offering" (141:2) Revelation 5:8 and 8:3–5 express a similar understanding of incense.

In Catholic worship, incense symbolizes our prayers rising up to God. It's used in settings where thanksgiving or adoration of God is emphasized.

While Orthodox, Lutheran, and Anglican (Episcopalian) Christians also use incense in their worship, many other Protestant traditions avoid it. Some even vilify the practice, but this doesn't mean there's no biblical basis for it. It can be an aid to worship and help us visualize what we do when we pray.

How many different forms of the Mass are there?

Seven rites are recognized by the Catholic Church: Latin, Byzantine, Alexandrian, Syriac, Armenian, Maronite, and Chaldean. These liturgical traditions have their origins in three ancient Christian centers: Rome, Antioch, and Alexandria. Yet these seven rites are in fact liturgical "families" in which accepted variations can be found.

Within the Latin rite, the Roman rite is used by the vast majority of Catholics around the world. However, three local liturgical traditions are approved for use—the Mozarabic (Archdiocese of Toledo, Spain), the Ambosian (Archdiocese of Milan, Italy), and the Bragan (Archdiocese of Braga, Portugal)—and three religious orders have permitted liturgical rites: Dominican, Carmelite, and Carthusian.

The Byzantine rite has twelve variations with origins in three languages (Greek, Old Slovanic, and Romanian). The Alexandrian rite has come to us from two ancient African languages: Coptic and Ge'ez (the language of ancient Ethiopia). The two forms of the ancient Chaldean rite originated in regions we now call Iraq and India. A version of the Syriac rite (Malankarese) also has its origins in India. The Armenian rite comes from the first kingdom to embrace Christianity (early 300s). The Maronite rite is the only liturgical tradition with origins in Aramaic, the language Jesus spoke in ancient Palestine.

The breadth and variety of these liturgical traditions—with origins on three different continents—express the richness of a Church that encompasses regions, cultures, and languages from around the world.

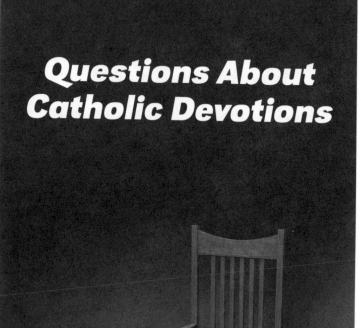

Questions About
Catholic Devotions

Why do Catholics pray to Mary and the saints?

I enjoy answering this question because the answer brings so much comfort.

Many Protestants dislike the way Catholics invoke Mary and the saints when offering prayers in times of need or moments of thanksgiving. After all, Jesus Christ is our one mediator; prayers should be directed to him, not his mother or the saints.

Catholics agree with Protestants that we neither have nor need any mediator other than Jesus Christ. Prayers made in the name of Jesus or the Trinity are effective—we don't need intercessors. But the Church is not simply made up of the living—it includes all who have believed and grown in holiness of thought and action. Therefore, from the early centuries of Christianity, Christians have sought the prayers of those who have passed through death and enjoy fellowship with God.

All Christians find comfort in the prayers of the living in times of great need or thanksgiving. Catholics (as well as Orthodox believers and some Anglicans) include Mary and the saints in this circle of fellowship. Their prayers do not stand between us and God; instead, they join with our prayers and become the prayers of the community of believers.

As I grew into the Catholic experience, this insight more than any other filled me with hope and expectation. My vision of the Church expanded, and I realized that even when I felt lonely and isolated the communion of saints was present to comfort and guide me. And while seeking the prayers of Mary and the saints is not required of those who become Catholic, I've found it to be one of the great comforts of my journey of faith.

Doesn't the Hail Mary address Jesus' mother as though she were a goddess?

It's important to look at the text of the Hail Mary and consider the sources used in composing it. Here is the most common English form, annotated to show the scriptural and historical basis for the text:

> Hail Mary, full of grace, The Lord is with thee. Blessed art thou among women *(Luke 1:28),* And blessed is the fruit of thy womb, Jesus *(Luke 1:42).* Holy Mary, Mother of God *(title given to Mary by the Council of Ephesus in 431),* pray for us sinners, now and at the hour of our death. Amen.
>
> COUNCIL OF TRENT, 1545–1563

This salutation (or petition) is grounded in Scripture and two Church councils. Because Mary is understood to hold a unique place in the communion of saints (see page 57), seeking her prayers feels very natural to Catholics. She is addressed as the Mother of God (see page 66) because she gave human flesh to the Son of God. She is not a goddess, but a human being who has a unique intimacy and relationship with God.

Doesn't Matthew 6:7 condemn methods of prayer like the rosary?

Jesus didn't intend to condemn formal prayer in this passage, which reads, "In praying, do not babble like the pagans, who think that they will be heard because of their many words." Otherwise, two verses later he wouldn't have taught his disciples the Lord's Prayer (Matthew 6:9–13). The concern appears to be with "Gentiles" who repeated words like they were magical charms.

The rosary is the result of a rich tradition of prayer and meditation. Drawing inspiration from 1 Thessalonians 5:17, to "pray without ceasing," early Christians used physical aids, including beads, to help them maintain a constant life of prayer. The English word *bead* comes from the Middle English word for *prayer.*

Today's rosary, which developed between the 1200s and 1500s, starts with a crucifix attached to a strand of beads which is attached to a circle of fifty-four beads. A specific prayer—the Apostles' Creed, Lord's Prayer, Glory Be, or Hail Mary—is assigned to each bead.

Each time we pray the rosary, we meditate on one of four aspects of Jesus' life and work called *Mysteries*: the Joyful Mysteries, five joyful events in Jesus' and Mary's lives; the Luminous Mysteries, five events that illuminate Jesus' mission; the Sorrowful Mysteries, Jesus' death and four events that occurred shortly before it; and the Glorious Mysteries, Jesus' resurrection and four events that followed it. We say ten Hail Marys for each event within the Mystery.

The rosary is a Bible-based, profoundly Christian form of meditation and prayer that has helped Catholics through the centuries stay focused and pray without ceasing. Mary is understood to be the petitioner's prayer partner, a reflection of the Catholic sense that we are surrounded by a communion of saints—especially Jesus' mother—who seek God's best for us.

Do Catholics really believe that people become sinless saints in this life?

Saints are not recognized because they were sinless during their earthly lives. They're recognized for exercising the Christian virtues to a heroic degree during their earthly lives. They illustrate the many ways we can live out the Christian faith.

In the early Christian communities, those who died for their faith—called *martyrs*—received special attention for their courage in the face of persecution. Those who survived persecution—called *confessors*—were admired because their stories encouraged Christians during 300 years of persecution.

After Christianity became the established religion of the Roman Empire, those who chose to give up the comforts of this world for a life of prayer and self-denial—like monks and nuns—were added to the list of spiritual heroes for the faithful to imitate. In recent centuries, the scope of those held up as examples has expanded. Pope John Paul II canonized more people than any other pope.

Unfortunately, saints' lives have often been presented in ways that almost deny their humanity and place them beyond our experience. Cardinal John Henry Newman, a great Anglican theologian who became Catholic in midlife, said, "I have no tendency to be a saint…I may be well enough in my way, but it is not the 'high line.'" He wrote some of the harshest critiques of Roman Catholicism imaginable during his Anglican years, yet Pope Benedict XVI beatified him in 2010, and he is now one level from sainthood.

These efforts are hopeful signs, for we need to know that the examples we're encouraged to follow were real people who struggled as we do. Their lives should encourage us and help us see that we too can be used by God, because God can redeem lives and use us for God's good purposes.

Why have Catholics focused on Jesus crucified rather than on Christ resurrected?

At times, Catholics have been accused of being obsessed with Jesus' gruesome death. Large images in churches portray Christ on the cross with Mary, Mary Magdalene, and John at his feet. Laypeople, nuns, and priests carry rosaries with crucifixes of Jesus' contorted body. In part, this happened because the Mass focused on Christ's suffering and death on the cross as the expiatory sacrifice for our sins. His death restored our relationship with God. The crucifix was an ever-present reminder of Christ's love for us.

In the 1970s, the focus on Jesus crucified seemed to shift, and a greater interest in the resurrected Christ was displayed in church art and devotions. The monastic community I later joined had added a fifteenth station of the cross—the resurrection. The parish I attended in Tuscaloosa, Alabama, had an image of the resurrected Christ above the altar instead of the crucified Savior.

The liturgy introduced after Vatican II shifted the focus of Catholic eucharistic celebration toward the Communion sacrifice at the Last Supper, when Christ identified with the paschal lamb (the Passover sacrifice) and enjoined his followers to eat his body and drink his blood under the signs of consecrated bread and wine (see pages 37–39). This focus on the Eucharist as a meal, celebrating our fellowship with God and receiving the spiritual nourishment needed to live the Christian life, has encouraged Catholics to focus on the resurrection and the new life that comes to us through Christ's death and resurrection.

Like the people of Israel, who were slaves in Egypt destined for destruction, we've been saved from spiritual death and strengthened in our journey of faith to reach the Promised Land—the kingdom of God.

Why are older Catholic churches filled with so many statues and pictures, while newer Catholic churches have very few?

Until the nineteenth century, most people didn't know how to read or write, and religious ideas were conveyed through visual representations. Around the year 600, Pope Gregory the Great cautioned that to adore or worship these objects violates the first commandment. However, he stressed that they should not be destroyed because they represent sacred events and saintly people and could be used to teach nonbelievers and illiterate Christians, who "read by looking at the walls what they cannot read in books."

In the 1500s, when the printing press made books more accessible and cheap, ordinary people learned to read and the Catholic Church used printed books. But statues and images remained a key way of learning about the faith.

In reaction to Protestant condemnations of this practice and promotion of learning about the faith from reading Scripture, some Church leaders expressed grave concerns about uneducated laypeople reading the Bible and discouraged this practice without the aid of a priest or catechist. This changed with Vatican II (1962–1965), and the *Catechism of the Catholic Church* now urges the faithful to regularly read the Bible (131–133). Therefore, Catholic churches continued to be filled with symbols of biblical events and Catholic saints.

Many Catholics no longer learn about their faith through images in churches. For that reason, not to mention the expense, Catholic churches built since 1960 have far fewer images and statues than churches built earlier.

How is the Catholic veneration of the consecrated host not an abuse of the Eucharist?

During the first thousand years of Christianity, the consecrated bread of the Eucharist became such a source of spiritual strength and comfort that parishes, monasteries, and even hermits maintained a small supply of consecrated bread for use when someone was sick or near death. Because the consecrated bread was understood to be Christ's Body mystically made present at the eucharistic celebration, the places where these supplies were stored became spaces where the faithful came to pray and meditate on Christ's continued presence in the world through the "blessed sacrament."

In the 1000s, an archdeacon in France questioned whether Christ was physically present under the signs of bread and wine. He and others began to speak of the "eucharistic Christ," implying that the Christ of the Gospels was not really present in the Eucharist.

Over the next 200 years, western Christians struggled to find language to talk about this sacramental mystery. This resulted in the use of the term *transubstantiation* to explain how Christ could be present in the Eucharist even though the elements continued to look, taste, and feel like bread and wine (see pages 38–39).

During the 1500s, in the wake of Protestant rejection of the doctrine of transubstantiation, exposition of the Blessed Sacrament became a way for Catholics to affirm their faith in Christ's presence in the Eucharist. While Protestants condemn this devotional practice as idolatry and even use derogatory terms like "cookie worship" to describe the practice, it is in fact a powerful way for Catholics to take time to reflect on how Christ loves us and continues to be present to us in the sacrament of the Eucharist.

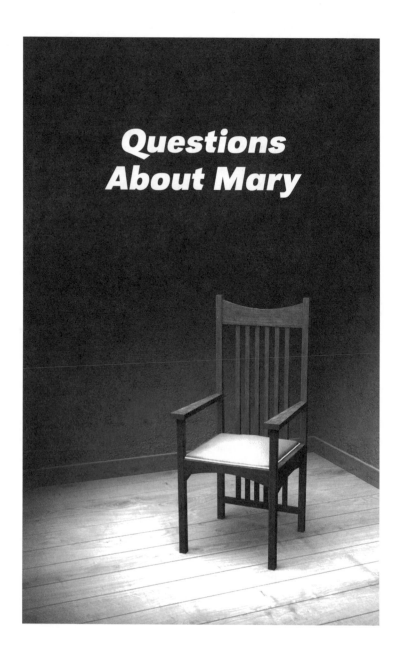

Questions
About Mary

How does Mary fit into the Catholic faith?

Shortly after I became Catholic, a good friend and his wife invited me to dinner. He was an Anglican preparing for ordination and very evangelical in his outlook. Conversation was polite and tactful until after dessert, when my friend explained that they wanted to understand why I had become Catholic. He hesitantly asked, "What do you think about Mary?" I smiled and responded, "I think she's wonderful, don't you?" He responded with an embarrassed "Yes, but…."

If Catholics and Protestants can begin with this premise—that Mary is wonderful—it might be possible to step back and consider why. Mary is an extraordinary human being who holds a special place in the Christian faith for two reasons: first, it was through her that God became flesh in the person of Jesus Christ; and second, she was the first to believe in Jesus' mission and ministry.

All Catholic doctrine about Mary refers to two special relationships. She has a special relationship with God because she bore the "God-man" in her womb. She also has a special relationship with us because she was the first Christian.

When Catholics call Mary the Mother of God, isn't that another way of saying she is a goddess?

No, it's a way to remind us that Jesus (the divine Son of God) took human flesh (was incarnated) from Mary. The title Mother of God (*Mater Dei*) is an imprecise translation of the Greek title *Theotokos*, which literally means "God-bearer," or "the one who gives birth to God."

Around 430 the patriarch of Constantinople, Nestorius, asserted that Mary should be called the *Christotokos* ("Christ-bearer," or "the mother of Jesus' humanity only"). Some Church leaders worried that this might lead Christians to think that Jesus' personhood could be divided, as though his human nature and his divine nature had not united.

For Christian leaders like Cyril of Alexandria, this distinction sabotaged the fullness of the incarnation and made it harder to understand the nature of our salvation. The Council of Ephesus was called to resolve this and other doctrinal issues. In 431 the council gave Mary the title *Theotokos* to clarify two issues. One is that Jesus is one person who is both God and man. The other is that Jesus is the incarnated Son of God (the enfleshed Word of God) who entered the created order to live among us, experience the brokenness of our world, and—through his suffering, death, and resurrection—redeem the world and each of us.

Over the last 500 years, some Protestants have become disconnected from this historical understanding of Mary's title. It seems to them that Catholics, Orthodox, and certain Protestants are trying to deify Mary, but this is not the case.

Why do Catholics believe in the immaculate conception of Mary?

This Catholic doctrine affirms that from the moment of her existence, Mary received grace normally received at baptism: preserved from original sin and infused with sanctifying grace. This immaculate conception of Mary should not be confused with the miraculous conception of Jesus.

Christians referred to Mary as "spotless" or "immaculate" by the 400s. In the late 1000s an Englishman named Eadmer (1064–1124) wrote the first tract explaining the doctrine of Mary's immaculate conception. His explanation met with opposition from influential Church leaders and theologians over the next 200 years. The debate extended over centuries.

In 1854, Pope Pius IX declared the Immaculate Conception of Mary to be a settled dogma of the Church in a document entitled God Ineffable (*Ineffabilis Deus*). The document appealed to Scripture (Genesis 3:15, Luke 1:28, and Song of Songs 4:7) as well as Church Tradition.

Why do Catholics believe in Mary's assumption into heaven?

Mary's assumption—body and soul—to heaven is a belief shared by Eastern Christians and Roman Catholics, although the explanations of this Marian dogma have different emphases in the two traditions. While there is no biblical or early historical record of this event, the first explanation of this doctrine is found in a document from the late 300s. As the centuries progressed, it became part of Marian teaching throughout the Christian world.

Sixteenth-century Protestant reformers rejected this teaching along with most of Catholic devotion focused on Mary. Among today's Protestant traditions, only in parts of the Anglican communion can one still find devotion to this and other beliefs about Mary.

Mary's assumption was considered a pious opinion until 1950, when Pius XII defined it as dogma (official teaching of the Church). The pope made the declaration after he and Church bishops found overwhelming consensus throughout the Church.

Pius XII settled this question in the wake of the devastating second world war and in the midst of the precarious Cold War. In the face of cruel disregard for human dignity and the callous abuse of human bodies, it was tempting to question the value of a human life or the goodness of the body.

The definition of Mary's assumption—body and soul—to heaven reaffirmed that God had not only created humans but also redeemed them and claimed them. The dogma of Mary's assumption reminded the world in bleak times of the goodness of God's creation and that Christ redeems us from the evil around us (and in us) and made us a new creation.

But perhaps the best explanation can be found in Pope John Paul II's 2004 homily at Lourdes. In it he quoted John 14:3, "And if I go and prepare a place for you, I will come back again and take you to myself, so that where I am you also may be." The pope explained that Mary's assumption is the pledge that Christ's promise will be fulfilled. The pope's words echo the teaching of bishops at Vatican II, which described this dogma as "a sign of sure hope and solace" (*Lumen Gentium*, 68).

Do Catholics believe Mary is co-Redemptrix?

Mary as co-Redemptrix is not an official teaching of the Catholic Church, although it is a pious opinion that has been part of Marian devotion for centuries. While Pope John Paul II cherished this opinion, Pope Benedict XVI has described it as problematic, and Vatican II documents don't include it among the titles attributed to Mary.

Catholics believe that Christ is the only Redeemer of humankind, and our salvation can be achieved only through this work (1 Timothy 2:5). Mary herself required the redemption provided by Christ's work on the cross. This Christian truth is shared by Protestants and Catholics.

Reflections on Mary's cooperation in Christ's redemptive work date back at least to the 100s. Devotees of Mary as co-Redemptrix emphasize that the she is not "co-equal" with Christ in the work of redemption, but a co-worker with him. Her response at the Annunciation, when she said yes to the call given her by Gabriel, makes her a co-worker in the redemption of humankind (Luke 1:38). Her sufferings at the foot of the cross are also emphasized, and devotees treat this as the fulfillment of Simeon's prophecy to Mary, "and you yourself a sword will pierce" (Luke 2:35).

Pope Benedict believes many find the opinion confusing and that it contains ideas that are already articulated better in other Marian doctrines. So while many millions of Catholics will continue to reflect on the mysteries found in this way of reflecting on Mary, this opinion is not shared by all Catholics.

Do Catholics believe Mary deserves the title Mediatrix of Graces?

This is another title that is widely accepted among Catholics and cherished by some popes but is not part of the dogmatic teaching of the Catholic Church.

Protestants assume it means Mary shares with Jesus the role of mediator between God and humankind. This is not true. Catholics and Protestants share the belief that there is only one mediator, and he is Jesus Christ (1 Timothy 2:5; *Lumen Gentium*, 62).

Catholic use of this title reflects a profound belief in the communion of saints and the intercession of the saints on our behalf. The Church is made up of the living and the dead. If we can ask for the prayers of living believers, how much more should we seek out the prayers of the faithful departed?

This is above all true for Mary, who holds a unique place among humans as the mother of Jesus Christ. Her participation in the work Christ accomplished in his life on Earth and her profound connection as his mother give her a special place when Catholics seek the prayers of the saints.

Yet this confidence in Mary's role in intercessory prayer should never be mistaken for a belief that she has a mediating role alongside or apart from Christ. It is even misleading to describe this as a role "with and under" Christ, for it suggests that this is somehow apart from him. Rather, Mary is the preeminent example of one who is immersed in Christ and whose work flows from him. Only in this way can we understand Mary as mediatrix. She is not a substitute for Jesus, who is our only mediator before God the Father.

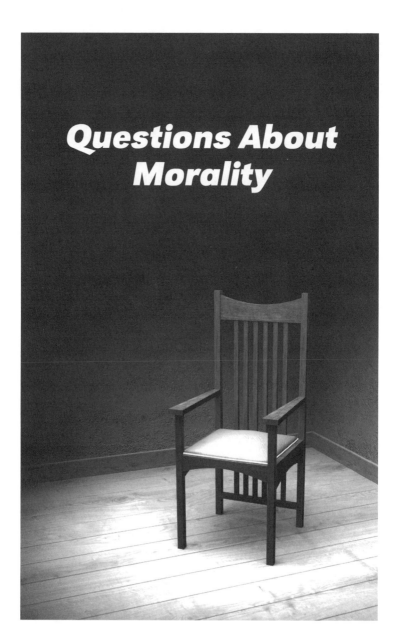

Questions About Morality

Why do the pope and the Catholic bishops tell married people how to live?

The simple answer is that the pope and the bishops are responsible for teachings that relate to faith and morals, just like the pastor of a Protestant church is responsible for guiding his congregation by teaching what is true to the tradition of his community. Catholics believe that Jesus commissioned Peter and the apostles, and consequently their successors, with the mission to teach, govern, and sanctify the faithful. As such, their mission as leaders in the Church constitutes a sacred responsibility entrusted to them by God.

An added crucial dimension is that Catholics believe the pope and the bishops receive their authority through apostolic succession, the generations going all the way back to the original apostles. This spiritual claim gives their judgments a special authority.

Directions from Church leaders touch the most intimate aspects of married life. Popes and bishops rely on the Word of God in sacred Scripture, guidance of the Holy Spirit in sacred Tradition, long-standing teaching on faith and morals, and learned considerations of Catholic theologians to promote a fuller understanding of committed love. Their judgments are conservative in the most technical sense of the word, that is, conserving/preserving the teaching and practice of previous generations of Christians.

In other words, they're doing what a pastor of any Christian community should—preserving the truth as the community has understood it.

Do Catholics really practice what the pope and the bishops teach?

Like the members of any religion, Catholics respond to the teachings of their leaders in different ways. Some obey every rule and recommendation. Others question everything and aren't satisfied with the answers. Still others study the issues and, after prayer and reflection, decide that in conscience they agree—or disagree—with their leaders on controversial questions of moral or doctrinal teaching. But no matter what their response, Catholics do not disregard or lightly ignore Church teaching.

In areas of life where new possibilities come to light, it can take years, decades, or even centuries to reach a clear and common view of how to proceed based on Scripture, Jesus' teachings, and a clear understanding of the moral truths at stake. Were those who dissented from the teachings of those Church leaders in their own time "good Catholics"? Were leaders who made the best judgment they could in their own time—a judgment the Church now teaches is wrong—"bad Catholics"? Here is where Christ's Law of Love must guide us. Church leaders, theologians, and laypeople condemned by Church decisions in their own time have sometimes been vindicated by later judgments.

Neither unthinking obedience nor stubborn resistance to inconvenient teaching is the response of mature Christians. Becoming truly informed about one's faith, learning what Church leaders teach about difficult matters, and making a prayerful judgment on how to respond are the best ways to engage the difficult questions, challenges, and possibilities Catholics confront.

Must non-Catholic spouses agree to raise their children as Roman Catholics?

According to the Catholic Church's 1983 *Code of Canon Law*, Catholics who receive permission from Church leaders to marry a non-Catholic promise to do all in their power to baptize and raise their children as Roman Catholics (1125). Only the Catholic spouse is expected to make this commitment.

This is a delicate, often painful question, especially if the non-Catholic is devout in practicing another faith tradition. It is best to search out those who are experienced in marriage preparation to explore the implications of this issue.

Can Catholics get divorced?

It isn't possible for anyone—including the Church, a pope, a bishop, or priest—to break a sacramentally bound marriage. The Church teaches that God joins a couple who freely unites in holy matrimony with unbreakable spiritual bonds. No earthly power can undo what God has joined. A couple may civilly divorce and separate, but if the marriage was sacramentally bound, they remain married in the eyes of God and the Church.

Civilly divorced Catholics who don't remarry remain in good standing with the Church. In 1981, Pope John Paul II said that the whole Church must help divorced people understand that they are not excluded and remain part of the Church (On the Role of the Christian Family in the Modern World [*Familiaris Consortio*], 84).

Those who remarry without an annulment, which results from an investigation of the sacramental character of their first marriage, are considered to be in a state of separation from the Eucharist communion. These people, while still expected to attend Mass every week and adhere to Church teaching, are understood to have broken the unity of the Church and must abstain from receiving the Eucharist.

Annulments in the Catholic Church consider the spiritual character of the marriage. Did the two people in the relationship understand the sacramental ministry of Catholic marriage? Did they enter into that sacramental covenant freely? If the answer to either of these questions is no, the marriage isn't considered sacramental. That doesn't mean the marriage was illicit or that children weren't the fruit of a civilly legitimate union. It does mean that no *sacramental* union took place.

When this has been established and an annulment granted, the people are free to enter into a sacramental marriage and continue to receive the Eucharist.

What do Catholics believe about homosexuality?

It is crucial to understand that Catholics make a distinction between homosexual orientation and homosexual acts.

The magisterium teaches that homosexual orientation is fundamentally disordered because it is understood to be contrary to the human being's nature as male and female. However, the magisterium does not teach that people who have a homosexual orientation have sinned—they haven't. The magisterium teaches that only people who knowingly and willingly choose to engage in homosexual acts are committing sin. Catholics are called to demonstrate love and compassion for their homosexual sisters and brothers, but the magisterium condemns all homosexual acts as immoral and "gravely contrary to chastity"(Catechism of the Catholic Church, 2396).

In 1986, the Congregation for the Doctrine of the Faith, led by then-Cardinal Joseph Ratzinger (now Pope Benedict XVI), issued a strongly worded call for civility and respect for homosexual persons. *On the Pastoral Care of Homosexual Persons* emphasized, "It is deplorable that homosexual persons have been and are the object of violent malice in speech or in action. Such treatment deserves condemnation from the Church's pastors wherever it occurs." The 1995 *Catechism* repeated these admonitions, stressing that homosexuals "must be accepted with respect, compassion and sensitivity" (2358).

In 1997 the United States Conference of Catholic Bishops issued a document titled *Always Our Children*. It explains that "a homosexual orientation cannot be considered sinful, for morality presumes the freedom to choose." The bishops went on to observe, "Sexual identity helps to define the unique persons we are, and one component of our sexual identity is sexual orientation."

Questions About Catholic Teaching

Why are there Catholic and Protestant versions of the Bible?

This fascinating story starts with the Protestant Reformation and stretches back into the early centuries of Christianity.

Martin Luther translated the Bible into German and developed strong views about the "canon of Scripture," the texts that should be included in the Bible as inspired by God. His conclusions emerged from study of ancient copies of Scripture, the opinions of other Christian scholars of his era, and the great ancient Bible translator Saint Jerome (c.340–420). Luther decided that seven Old Testament books should be removed from the canon and puzzled over the removal of four New Testament books (Hebrews, James, Jude, and Revelation).

While Luther's views about the New Testament books didn't win the support of his followers, his conclusions about the Old Testament became the consensus of sixteenth-century Protestants. Luther's conclusion rested on two factors: 1) the consensus of Jewish rabbis to exclude certain texts from the Hebrew Bible, and 2) the opinion of Saint Jerome, which was based on the decisions of those rabbis.

Christians had been using a Greek translation of the Hebrew Bible completed more than 100 years before the birth of Jesus. Called the *Septuagint*, this collection of Jewish Scriptures included texts that had been composed in Greek, not Hebrew. Because the *Septuagint* had been used during the time of Jesus and in the early decades of Christianity, Christians came to view that Greek translation as the version of the Jewish Scriptures that should be trusted as inspired.

At the end of the first century and into the next, Jewish leaders decided that Jews should accept only texts written in Hebrew as part of their canon of Scripture. This meant that seven books from the *Septuagint* were excluded.

In the late 300s and early 400s, Jerome translated the Old Testament into Latin from the Hebrew texts rather than from the *Septuagint* (Greek) texts. His translation eventually became the standard text used by Christians in western Europe.

Luther sided with Jerome's conclusions about the Hebrew Bible and excluded the seven books found in the *Septuagint* that had been rejected by the rabbis, but Jerome's attempts to convince Church leaders to exclude them were unsuccessful. Therefore, Catholics have seven more Old Testament books than Protestants.

If Luther had his way, the New Testament might have four fewer books as well. So historically, the Catholic version of the Bible is the one that most Christians have accepted since the earliest centuries of Christianity. The Protestant Bible is shorter because Martin Luther and his supporters followed the decision of the second-century rabbis and the opinion of Jerome.

One thing everyone agrees on is that there is only one Bible—there are different versions and translations of that Bible, but there is only one Bible.

FURTHER READING

Joseph T. Lienhard, *The Bible, The Church, And Authority* (Liturgical Press, 1995).

Do Catholics have to believe what the Pope says?

Catholics believe the pope has a responsibility to lead Catholics in their faith and practice and that what he says carries great weight and should never simply be ignored. But Catholics are not bound to believe *everything* he says. In *Jesus of Nazareth* (Doubleday, 2007), Pope Benedict XVI says, "This book is in no way an exercise of the magisterium, but is solely an expression of my personal search…. Everyone is free, then, to contradict me. I would only ask my readers for that initial goodwill without which there can be no understanding." The pope views his official documents in a different way (for they often deal with doctrine and Christian practice), so his statement is a helpful reminder that the context in which he speaks is always important. Of course, when the pope speaks ex cathedra ("from the chair" of Saint Peter), he is understood to teach with authority received from Christ (see pages 4 and 19).

Many theologians and diocesan leaders are laypeople. In the absence of priests, laypeople provide pastoral care in parish communities. The *Code of Canon Law* states that laypeople "have the right and even at times the duty to manifest to the sacred pastors their opinion on matters which pertain to the good of the Church" (212). This is an important point to keep in mind when we're tempted to think lay Catholics have no voice in the life of the Church.

Catholics should never simply ignore what the pope teaches on faith and Christian practice, but as the current pope reminds us, at times we are free to disagree and debate ideas expressed by popes. Indeed, canon law makes it clear that at times we have a duty to do just that.

However, we must never forget that the pope's role is to lead us into a true understanding of the faith and how we should live it. We ignore his conclusions and directions at our peril.

What role does Scripture play in the life of Catholics?

Scripture is at the center of Catholic worship. As a curious young Protestant, the first thing I noticed about Catholic Masses was that they include readings from the Old Testament, the Psalms, the New Testament, and the Gospels. In the Christian tradition I grew up in, the pastor would often preach long sermons around a fragment of one verse. It seemed that Catholics took Scripture far more seriously than Protestants because they read more of it in their worship.

This impression was reinforced when I got to know a monastic community. Many times a day, the community and guests gathered in the chapel for short services where they sang psalms, read portions of the Bible, and reflected on what they had heard. The centrality of the Scriptures deeply impressed me and made me aware that my assumptions about Catholics and their use of the Bible did not match reality.

I later learned about the *Breviary*. This collection of Bible readings, prayers, and hymns can be done alone, with family, or with a prayer group. Here, again, Catholics had a well-developed and long practice of reading and reflecting on the Scriptures.

Before Vatican II, Catholic leaders often discouraged laypeople from reading and interpreting the Bible on their own. This attitude had developed, in part, because of Protestant and Catholic tensions since the Reformation. This changed with Vatican II. The *Catechism of the Catholic Church* now urges the faithful to regularly read the Bible (131–133), and in most parishes today you will find Catholic Bible studies and laypeople who strive to educate themselves about the Bible and how it applies to their lives.

How can you accept teachings that are not in the Bible?

Catholics believe that divine revelation is both written and unwritten. The Bible (God's written revelation) cannot be separated from Tradition (God's unwritten revelation), because the Bible itself is a product of Tradition. It didn't just drop from heaven. It came to us through the experience and traditions of Christians in the earliest generations of the Church. This profound truth is the starting point for Catholics.

Catholics trust that the teachings handed down through the generations reflected the lived and living faith of Christians. We accept that later generations of believers asked questions that required clarification and definition. The existence and nature of purgatory, doctrines related to Mary, the nature of papal authority, and many more questions have required theologians, bishops, and popes to discern the truth. When dealing with these issues, Scripture is the essential starting point, but it is never the final stop. The living experience of the Church and its leaders also plays a role.

This isn't likely to be an area in which Catholics and Protestants agree. One of the founding principles of the Protestant movement was Martin Luther's assertion that doctrine should be determined only by the Bible (*sola scriptura*). In response, the Council of Trent (1545–1563) insisted that Church teaching is based on both the Bible and Tradition.

This honest difference must be acknowledged and understood.

What does the Catholic Church teach about miracles?

For well over 200 years, miracles have been dismissed as impossible. In the 1700s, faith in human reason and the laws of nature dismissed miraculous accounts in the Bible and Christian tradition. Yet in recent decades, people of faith are more willing to recognize that God's engagement in human history can be achieved in the context of humanity's quest to understand the world created by God.

The Bible has no word for miracles, instead identifying signs, wonders, or works of power. While Jesus' ministry included healings, exorcisms, and extraordinary events that defied the natural order, parallel stories existed in ancient Mediterranean cultures, and early Christians accepted them as signs of the coming of the kingdom of God (Matthew 12:28; Luke 11:20). Faith that God works wonders proved key for those affected (Matthew 8:5–13 and 15:21–28; Mark 5:21–43, 9:14–29, and 10:46–52; Luke 17:11–19).

This connection is central to the Catholic understanding of miracles. While verification that an event is unexplainable may be sought from experts, their judgments alone don't prove divine contravention of the natural order. Much more important is the relationship with God that grows from that event.

These signs, wonders, and works of power are existential experiences of God in human history. They cannot be scientifically proven or replicated. They are by their very nature unique moments of God's presence in the world and of the kingdom of God.

FURTHER READING
Catechism of the Catholic Church, 547–550

Does the practice of indulgences continue?

Indulgences have been a matter of great controversy and misunderstanding for over 500 years. Protestant reformers quite rightly reacted to abuses associated with the granting of indulgences in the early 1500s. But the polemics of the Reformation hardened positions and entrenched misconceptions.

When a Catholic goes to a priest for the sacrament of reconciliation, three dimensions of the penitent's experience are required for the sacrament to be valid: The person must, in this order, 1) confess the fault to the priest; 2) be contrite and determined not to commit the act again; and 3) after receiving assurance from the priest that God has forgiven the sin, must perform a penitential act prescribed by the priest. The penitential act can't be performed before absolution is received. The penitential act doesn't earn the forgiveness, but addresses the temporal penalty associated with the sin.

In the early centuries of Christianity, temporal penalties could be onerous and lengthy for serious sins (like murder). Christians assumed that God required some form of retributive punishment for violations of God's laws even after the sin had been confessed and forgiven. As the centuries progressed, western European Christians determined that temporal penalties for forgiven sins not addressed in this life must be paid in purgatory.

Popes claimed their prerogative to use the merits accrued by the Christ and the communion of saints to mitigate these temporal penalties, preparing the living for a peaceful death and mitigating the suffering of the dead in purgatory.

Between the 1100s and 1400s, indulgences were granted only to those who participated in the Crusades or who attended the dedication of certain churches and church anniversaries. By the late 1400s and early 1500s, this practice had devolved into the unrestricted sale of indulgences. Corrupt practices led to false claims and scandalous behavior by professional "pardoners." In the wake of the Reformation and denunciations by Protestant reformers and Catholic leaders, Pope Pius V banned these types of indulgences.

In 1967, Pope Paul VI significantly revised the practical application of granting indulgences. The number a person could receive was greatly reduced and the purpose clarified. He emphasized that indulgences are effective only with true conversion of the heart.

The seeking of indulgences has declined in recent decades, and they are sought only by certain portions of the faithful. One reason may be that in many parts of the Church the faithful are encouraged to reflect on sin as a spiritual malady that needs the healing love of God rather than as a "legal" transgression that requires retributive justice.

Do all Catholics have to believe the same things?

Catholics affirm a deposit of faith that the Church has received and is bound to preserve. This includes the public revelation of God manifest in the incarnate Word of God (Jesus Christ) and preserved in the sacred Scriptures and apostolic Tradition. This deposit of faith ended with the death of the last apostle.

Catholics are not required to believe in many of the private revelations and visions that have accumulated over the centuries. Different spiritualities function side by side in the Roman Catholic Church and rightly claim to be a part of the Catholic tradition. But even when these revelations and visions are sanctioned and promoted by bishops and pope, they are not part of the deposit of faith.

It's complicated, because the deposit of faith entrusted to the Church is not simply a set of propositional truths, but is bound up in the person of Jesus Christ, who is the fullness of God's revelation to humanity. Catholics commonly agree on certain teachings central to the deposit of faith and taught by Church authority, including the life, death, and resurrection of Jesus Christ; the role of the sacraments in the life of the believer; and creeds formulated by ancient councils.

Since the mid 1800s, theologians and Church leaders continue to debate the infallible nature of documents issued by popes and Vatican and the extent to which they're binding on Catholics. All agree, however, that the laity should give these documents the utmost consideration and respect.

FURTHER READING
Francis O'Sullivan, *Magisterium: Teaching Authority in the Catholic Church* (Paulist Press, 1983).

Why do Catholics pray for people who have died?

People who have died are part of the Christian family, the communion of saints. Catholics believe that the dead, especially the recently deceased, can experience consolation and spiritual support from our prayers on their behalf.

We all have unfinished business at death—no one dies perfect and sinless in the sight of God. While grace and forgiveness is extended to those who have faith in Jesus Christ, Christians have long puzzled about how the departed are prepared to enter into the presence of God. Since earliest Christianity, believers have asked God to give grace and mercy to those passing through the purgation (purification) needed to be ready for union with God. Drawing on imagery from Scripture (Zechariah 13:9; Malachi 3:1–18; 1 Peter 1:7), Saint Augustine distinguished between the "refiner's fire" that "burned away" dross and prepared one for heaven and the eternal consuming fire intended for the unrepentant (Revelation 21:8).

From the 1000s forward, western European Christians referred to this experience as *purgatory*, a "place" between heaven and hell. Easing this suffering became an obsession for European Christians in the 150 years after the Black Death (1347–1351), when one third of Europe's population died gruesomely in a few short years. Protestant reformers of the 1500s rightly questioned the preoccupation and fear that accompanied practices Church leaders used to alleviate that anxiety—indulgences, for example (see page 86).

More recently, Cardinal John Henry Newman's imagining of purgatory, "The Dream of Gerontius" (1865), captures the sense of the biblical texts that inspired Augustine's reflections. As the soul of Gerontius is drawn irresistibly toward the searing love of God that purifies, the prayers of the living ease his way and are a source of consolation. That is why Catholics pray for the dead.

Don't most Catholics simply go through the motions?

I heard this many times during my years as a Protestant and even made the accusation myself. "They call themselves Catholic, but look at the way they live!" Or "They think going to Mass every Sunday makes them Christians."

This accusation can be hurled at any Christian group, for all denominations and community churches are made up of human beings who fall short of the Christian ideal. We understand ourselves to be a community of sinners saved by God's grace. In our baptism we have been claimed for God, and that calling marks us for life. That it takes more time for some than for others to respond to God's love is one of the mysteries of each faith journey.

Shortly before I was received into the Catholic Church, an Anglo-Irish friend expressed grave concerns. He had been baptized Catholic as an infant and confirmed as a teenager, but he hadn't been to Mass for fifteen years. He said, "Ken, when you become Catholic, you can never resign!"

Though my friend found this troubling, it proved a great comfort for me and a confirmation that I was doing the right thing. Someone who had strayed far from his spiritual roots still understood that he had a spiritual home. He had been claimed by God's grace in his baptism and confirmation. While the Catholic Church does take the task of educating and nurturing faith seriously, we recognize that our salvation begins in this life and is perfected in the next.

What does it mean to be a "good Catholic" or a "bad Catholic"?

Evangelical Protestants are understandably suspicious of both terms. Often people who use these self-assessments appear to be thinking about the things they do—or don't do. That's a fair criticism and a problem for some Catholics.

Like Christians in all traditions, some Catholics seek to save themselves through their own works. Yet there is another dimension of these terms that I find reassuring. People who are baptized into the faith know they have a spiritual home.

Like the prodigal son, "bad Catholics" may try to run away and waste their lives in ways that harm themselves and others. But God is waiting for their return and will receive them with love.

On the other hand, "good Catholics" should be cautious that they don't behave like the older brother in Christ's parable. Angry and resentful of the father's love for the wayward younger brother, the older brother exposed his resentment over service given out of duty (or desire for reward) and not love.

Conclusion

Where do I go from here?

This is a starting point, not an ending point. For a more comprehensive one-volume reference on doctrinal and moral teaching, pick up the *Catechism of the Catholic Church*. If you're facing questions about Catholic moral teachings and their application, Daniel L. Lowery's *Following Christ: How to Live a Moral Life* (Liguori Publications, 1996) is a great resource.

For questions about divorce and annulments, read Dennis and Kay Flowers' *Catholic Annulment, Spiritual Healing* (Liguori, 2002). Lawrence E. Mick's *How We Worship: The Eucharist, the Sacraments, and the Hours* (Liguori, 2009) is helpful for people who want more information on how to explain the Catholic Church's worship, sacraments, and way of praying.

Should you want help describing biblical teaching from a Catholic perspective, read Oscar Lukefahr's *A Catholic Guide to the Bible* (Liguori, 1998). And Christopher M. Bellitto's *Church History 101: A Concise Overview* (Liguori, 2008) is an accessible history of the Catholic Church.

May God richly bless you in your faith journey. Remember that you're not alone on your spiritual quest. In addition to the ever-present Holy Spirit and our mediator Jesus Christ, Mary and the communion of saints are always ready to pray with and for us in times of need and joy. Through the sacraments of the Church, you have access to tangible experiences of God's presence in the world. These and all sacramental experiences are signs of God's love for us, and for the universe God created. The ministers of the Church (pope, bishops, priests, and deacons) and all the people of God are a resource to help and support your growth in faith.

You belong to a community of believers that stretches back 2,000 years. Trust that God's power and love (grace) can help you be the

Christian you desire to be. Never forget that God's kingdom is both here (because of us) and not yet (because all is not fulfilled). We must cooperate with God's grace and do what we are able to spread knowledge of God's love throughout the world.

Always remember that Christ's Law of Love trumps any temptation to win an argument or denounce those who have challenged you. Never forget that Jesus told his followers: "I give you a new commandment: love one another. As I have loved you, so you also should love one another. This is how all will know that you are my disciples, if you have love for one another" (John 13:34–35).

How you treat those who corner you is as important as the accuracy of the information you provide. Be Christ's ambassador of love, and you will live out the most important principle of your Catholic faith.

Kenneth L. Parker, PhD, grew up in the Wesleyan Church and received his master's degree in historical theology from Fuller Theological Seminary. He became a Roman Catholic during his doctoral studies in reformation history at Cambridge University. For five years, Dr. Parker was a Benedictine monk and a student of nineteenth-century Catholic history at the University of Fribourg, Switzerland. He has been a professor of historical theology at Saint Louis University since 1992.